A POEM

TRAVELED DOWN

MY ARM

poems and

drawings

ALICE WALKER

A POEM

TRAVELED DOWN

MY ARM

random house | new york

All rights reserved under International and Pan-American Copyright
Conventions. Published in the United States by Random House,
an imprint of the Random House Publishing Group, a division of
Random House, Inc., New York, and simultaneously in Canada
by Random House of Canada Limited, Toronto.

RANDOM HOUSE and colophon are registered
trademarks of Random House, Inc.

LIBRARY OF CONGRESS CATALOGING-IN-PUBLICATION DATA

Walker, Alice,
   A poem traveled down my arm: poems and drawings / by Alice Walker.
      p. cm.
   ISBN 1-4000-6163-6
      I. Title.
   PS3573.A425P64 2003
   81'.54—dc21   2003047070

The author is committed to preserving ancient forests and natural resources
and wishes to acknowledge Random House for printing this book on paper
that is 100 percent postconsumer recycled fibers and processed chlorine
free. For more information about Green Press Initiative and the use of
recycled paper in book publishing, visit www.greenpressinitiative.org.

Random House website address: www.atrandom.com

9 8 7 6 5 4 3 2 1

FIRST EDITION

Book design by Barbara M. Bachman

To water

Until grief is restored

in the West as

the starting place where

the man and woman

might find peace,

the culture will continue

to abuse and ignore

the power of water,

and in turn will be

fascinated with fire.

—Malidoma Patrice Somé,
THE HEALING WISDOM OF AFRICA

This is a strange little book. It is like a plant in one's garden whose seed was blown in by the wind.

The story of *A Poem Traveled Down My Arm* is this: After giving up writing altogether—after more than thirty years of writing, I thought it was time— I had written a book of poems, *Absolute Trust in the Goodness of the Earth,* while on retreat in Mexico. My editor asked me to pre-autograph "tip-in sheets" for the new volume, and sent me five hundred. Signing these sheets of paper, which would later be "tipped" into the book and bound, would save me time later on autographing copies of the book at bookstores; readers, I think, like to buy books that are autographed. So I sat down near a sunny window, and between cooking and gardening and traveling and so on, I signed all five hundred sheets. By now, my autograph has become a scrawl, illegible to anyone but myself, and so I've begun to think of it not as words, but as a design. I sent the signed sheets off. A few days or weeks later, I was asked to autograph another thousand. I came face-to-face with how boring it is to write one's own name. Unlike many people who are asked for autographs and who willingly give them no matter what else they might be doing, I will often refuse. Gently and graciously, usually. Or I will explain: No, I am on my way to the dentist, a funeral, grocery shopping, this is not a good time. By now I must have written my name a million times.

As I began signing sheets of the quite high stack of blank paper, my pen joined me in boredom at writing my name. It began to draw things instead. I was delighted. There was an elephant! A giraffe! A sun! A moon! Hair!

And at the same time, as if completely *over* the mundane task of writing my name, we, my pen and I, began to write poems.

I was working in the dining room and keeping an ear open to things cooking on the stove in the kitchen. Sometimes I would rush to stir the soup, and a poem would bubble up so quickly I had to forget the soup and rush back to write the poem. For a while I simply signed the drawings and left them in the stack. I thought: How sweet to offer this signed drawing to the person who buys this book, rather than a scrawled signature. But the poems and drawings started to form something that I thought I might like to experience myself, so I pulled them out of the stack.

I saw that the poems spoke a different poem-language than I usually use, which meant I was somewhere, within myself, new. The drawings reflected the fact that I don't know how to draw, and yet, like folk art all over the world, they had Life. Stuffing them under a cushion because they seemed awkward wouldn't work, because they did have this life; they would peek out.

And that, dear reader, is the story. Not all of it, of course. *Because.* It is really a story about exhaustion. About deciding to quit. About attempting to give up

what it is not in one's power to give up: one's connec-
tion to the Source. Being taught this lesson. Ultimately
it is a story about Creativity, the force that surges and
ebbs in all of us, and links us to the Divine.

In *A Poem Traveled Down My Arm* there is a poem
that goes like this:

What hair
we here!

Mandela
Douglass
Einstein

Between assassination
&
suicide
living
happily.

On the page following this poem there is a drawing
of their hair. Mandela's is a mandala of curled and

tightly spiraled rosettes, all happy to grow over and around one another. Frederick Douglass's hair, the mane of a man who would not be a slave and definitely would not be badly dressed once he was free, is an attitudinal, kinky fluff that hangs to his neck. It was white as snow during much of his life, and must have lit up every room he entered, like a moon. Einstein's mind-blown locks speak to the naturalness that true creativity demands. He had seen where we're headed: The Third World War may be fought with bombs, he declared, but the Fourth World War will be fought with sticks and stones. Or words to that effect. Hair care was the least of it. And so his hair defines the expression "every which a way."

Mandela a "terrorist," Mandela with a price on his head, or on any piece of him, in fact; Mandela in prison for twenty-seven years; Mandela with a free heart. Douglass the same: enslavement, refusal of enslavement, flight, resistance, rebellion. *Free heart.* Einstein different, but similar: He saw humanity's enslavement to its fear of itself, where such fear would lead. Still he enjoyed some very good days.

And so it can be with us. And so says the poem:

Between assassination

&

suicide

living

happily.

A POEM

TRAVELED DOWN

MY ARM

Because

you rubbed

my shoulder

last night

a poem

traveled down

my arm.

Living

this year

in

disaster:

How

is

it different?

No one

has

escaped

a

blessing.

There is

no God

but

Love

&

Helpfulness

is

Its

name.

Air

is God

& connects

us.

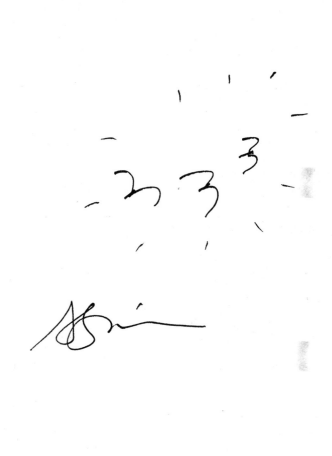

Every time

you

die

you live

differently.

You cannot

eat

money

&

if you could

it would

make

you

sick.

Removing

the

boulder

reveals

the

message

underneath.

Buddha

helps

us up

while

lying

down.

The right road

disappears

beneath

our

feet.

Goddess looks

through

your eyes

&

is

your hand.

The end

is coming

yesterday

it was

here

too.

Earth

is

too wet

to be

a

machine.

Those

who remember

have

been touched

by us.

Unload

the

useless

information

say

farewell

to

comparing

mind.

Balance

She is

not

dead

who left

her

giggle

in

your

empty

field.

You will

be

tried

in the

fires

of

small talk.

Your

suffering

from

witticisms

will

be

endless.

Fifty years

to see

the flower

at

my birth.

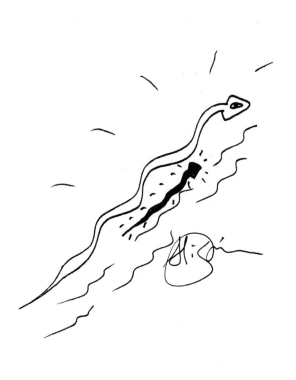

Snake

they

separated

us.

Feed

the

stranger

under

your

coat.

The dead

do not

have

long

to wait

for birth.

She

comes

from

heaven

unannounced.

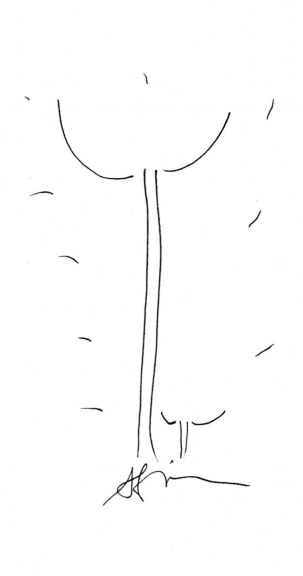

Birth

is

so

endless

Who

dies

being

born?

Love

your

friends.

We do not

know

anything

think

of that.

To remember

is

to plan.

River runs

from us;

Lake sees.

Mind

shine.

Leonard

was right

to

love

Virginia.

Virginia

was

right

to be

insane.

Who can

bear

to know

what evil

lurks

in our bowl

of peas?

Who is

in charge

loses.

Inflation

is

prelude.

A million

blessings

no one

home

in us.

What is

a promise

if

not

your

hand

in mine?

Fearless

lie down

beside me

I cannot

bite emptiness.

The straight

path

follows

an endless

curve.

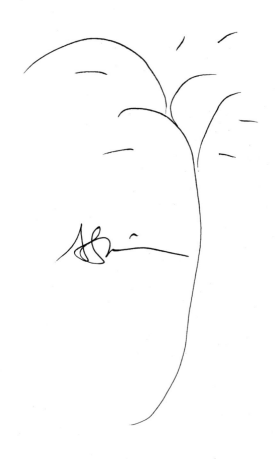

When we

have changed

everything

we will eat

congratulations

with

our tea.

No one

can end

suffering

except

through

dance.

Who dives

knows

water

ways.

Why not

choose?

What is

this

cradle

(of civilization)

but

the

grave?

Do not

cling

to being

lost.

What hair

we here!

Mandela

Douglass

Einstein

Between assassination

&

suicide

living

happily.

Understanding

war

I do not

harm

myself.

The Navy

so

loud

whales cannot

believe

our

silence.

Silent Spring

birds

&

even we

have lost

our

voice.

The crushed

teapot

in

the rubbish

of the

bulldozed

house

will sing

in your

ears

forever.

That is

the law.

The more

intelligence

the fewer

wars

&

children.

Not buying

war

grief

remains

unsold.

Neither

the war

nor

the

infant

was sent

to save

us

from

our

fate.

What do Indians dance

into

their dance?

Recognize

karma

y

el

destino.

Who taught us

to ask

for

that

which

makes

us

weep?

Why is

Earth

saying

yes, yes

smiling?

What do Africans

know

that

they

are

no longer

telling

us?

Mother Africa

turns

her head

away:

blood on

her

head

&

on

her

shoe.

She knows.

There is

no God

but

God

who closes

windows.

You will

long

for

me

&

I am

inside.

Her world

understands

us

as

The people who eat:

They who

bring

death.

You can buy

a piece

of

Antiquity

to impress

your

friends.

Half of it

was

crushed to dust

by Saviors

&

blew

away.

Civilization

was

an excuse.

Of what

do

Palestinians

dream

&

could we

live

there?

To live

in this world

is to accept

torture

even

of

tomatoes.

Who knew?

Not to have

faith—

Time is

too

long!

Release

the tyranny

of

white:

Paint your

house

to open

the heart

&

shelter

the soul;

eat

yams.

Release

the tyranny

of

black:

Worship

snow;

eat

escargot.

Release

the tyranny

of

gender:

Make

love

not

pro-

gramming.

Reborn

a

persimmon

tree

no mystery

how

to

behave.

But that

takes

Time.

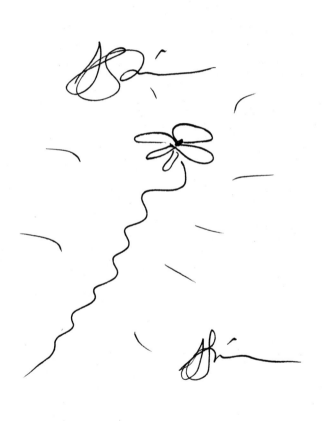

Buddha nature

not

a gift

from

Buddha

but

from

nature.

The living

die

when dead

men fight.

The old woman

sits beside

the window

that was

destroyed.

How can

you tell

she is

not you?

Know

the

notion

of bombing

you

was

no

friend

of

mine.

Who can dance

footless?

Woman

reborn

as

man

do

not forget

this life.

Man

reborn

as

woman

do not

give

in

to

fear.

Take a

risk—

grow old.

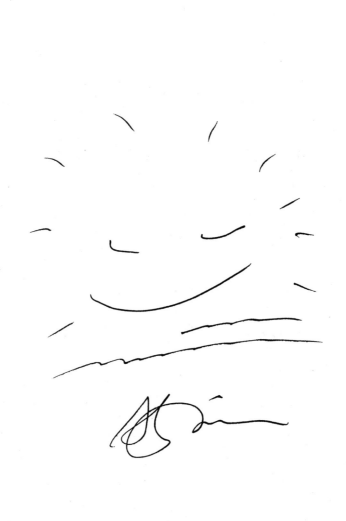

Kissing

Your

Arm

I kiss

The

Mountain.

Don't you

think

they

intend

to incinerate

the Earth

who create

a napalm

to burn

our flesh

even

under

water?

How long

we

have slept

dreaming

of getting

everywhere

some

where

faster.

In our

lifetime

no end

to

war.

What do birds

think

of

us?

Fleeting

thought

where

did

you

go?

Lost

poem.

When we die

the

ocean

of

Life

closes

over

us.

Do

not be

a

miracle

of

affliction

to

the

world.

Choose

someone

to love

who

wouldn't even

hear

of it.

Notice

ducks.

Children

trained

to

shoot

to kill

themselves:

We

the ground

on

which

they

fall.

Wear red.

How to hope

against

the evil

engulfing

us?

All around

our rented

pole house

in Paradise

acid lime

was laid

to

silence

frogs.

How can we

rest

thinking

of

their

burning

legs?

What is

the balm

for

consciousness?

There is only

kindness

lucid, strong

in the

moment

like   The offer

sunlight   of empathy

penetrating   or tea

a gloomy   or soup

glade   or

                        bread

                        a bed.

Lack

of balance

staggers

us.

To fall

is

easy.

Even so,

falling

will not

help.

No

gadget

in all

Creation

to

distract us

forever

from

our

grief.

We have seen

Paradise

over &

over

&

we have

lost

it

every

time.

Is it

the same

Paradise

we

lose

so constantly

in

ourselves?

There is

no

"Other"

only

you—

at

war.

For medicine

contemplate

a

breathing

leaf:

faithfulness.

Now

we know

why

models

we are

trained

to emulate

look

like

skeletons.

Stunning

It was not

Uranium

who chose

to be

our

enemy.

Depleted

She is

misunderstood

&

misused.

We are left

trailing

Her

footprints

which

last

forever.

Choose

one country

other

than

your

own

to love.

Keep a finger

on

its

pulse.

See

yourself

in every

eye

you

fear

to

look   You live

into.   there

                         and die

                         also.

                         Stop running.

Earth

Mother

will win

in the

end

absorb

us casually

&

grow

perfect

creations

from

our

mistakes.

Her

life

so long

can

start

over

&

over

again

without

us.

But

can I be

a flower

a weed

waving

&

blowing?

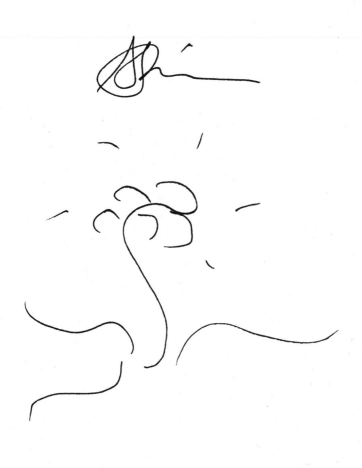

We are

protected

by

nothing

but

our

thoughts.

In

the land

where

all

is managed

the

opinion

of

the wise

arrives

by

accident.

Destroying

as it

builds

the serpent

swallows

its tail.

The tap

of

the hammer

the

whine

of

the

bomb.

Trying

to

explain

in

this

Age

of fragmentation

our

thoughts

disintegrate

on

the wind.

The poem

means—

but are they

good

shoes?

Is there

a

market

near

the

airport?

Is that

the

celebrity

the one

I love

or

the one

who died

along with all

her

dogs

&

two

giraffes?

Where is

Michael

when the lights

go out?

Respect

plutonium.

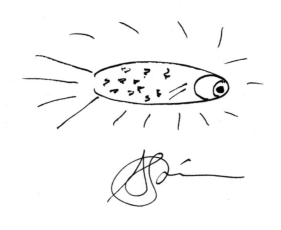

There is no end

to the

suffering

of

knowing   must

our   swim

species   in this toxic

is   sea

a   a shining fish

suicide: of

our   ill repute.

happiness

Lying in my lover's arms

there is a

smell

of

poi

that

steadies

me.

The luscious

papaya

too sweet

for

my body

not for

its

own.

Believe in

no God

that

does not

believe

in you.

Eat coco-

nuts.

Do not

repeat

everything

you've

learned.

You may be called upon

to lead.

Don't be

fooled

the

assaulted

child

is

ours

&

always

was.

I am not

so

easily

killed

as

you

thought:

So firmly

am I

a part

of

you.

You will

carry me

to

my resting

place

&

I will

leave

with

you.

Turn to the

wind

for

help.

Ask it

to drop

all radio-

active

particles

while

embracing

you.

There is

a swift

horse

whose name

is

Night.

Ride it

into

dreams.

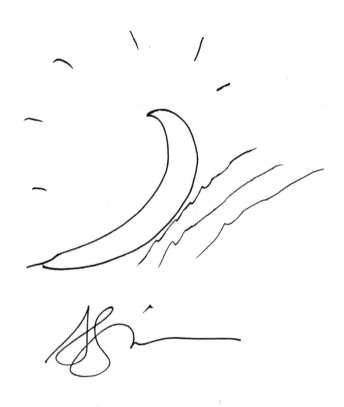

We must

dream

our

way

out

of this.

Strive

to remember

it is not

normal

to

live

in

terror

of

the water

in

your

glass.

Friendship

is

antidote

to

poison.

Do not

be

like

cows

grazing

watching

the

butcher.

If we are true

to Her

The Goddess

will come

to us.

She will

seem

odd.

And

I will go

on

blessing

old

revolutionaries

who

stand

their

ground

&

small

countries

that

never

give

up

I will go

on

believing

that

even

if

provoked

it is

inappropriate

to

bomb

teenagers

& that

infants

are not

to

blame

for fouling

their

societies

I will

go

on

believing

that

love

is

the future

that

I deserve

Peace

the future

whose

time

has

come.

About the Author

ALICE WALKER won the Pulitzer Prize and the American Book Award for her novel *The Color Purple,* which was preceded by *The Third Life of Grange Copeland* and *Meridian.* Her other bestselling novels include *By the Light of My Father's Smile, Possessing the Secret of Joy,* and *The Temple of My Familiar.* She is also the author of three collections of short stories, three collections of essays, six previous volumes of poetry, and several children's books. Her books have been translated into more than two dozen languages. Born in Eatonton, Georgia, Walker now lives in Northern California.